Uncles

by Lola M. Schaefer

Consulting Editor: Gail Saunders-Smith, Ph.D.

Consultant: Phyllis Edelbrock, First-Grade Teacher,
University Place School District, Washington

Pebble Books

an imprint of Capstone Press
Mankato, Minnesota

Pebble Books are published by Capstone Press
818 North Willow Street, Mankato, Minnesota 56001
http://www.capstone-press.com

Library of Congress Cataloging-in-Publication Data
Schaefer, Lola M., 1950–
  Uncles/by Lola M. Schaefer.
  p. cm.—(Families)
  Includes bibliographical references and index.
  Summary: Simple text and photographs depict uncles and what they can do
with their nieces and nephews.
  ISBN 0-7368-0261-4
  1. Uncles—Juvenile literature. [1. Uncles.] I. Title. II. Series: Schaefer, Lola M.,
1950–   Families.
HQ759.94.S35   1999
306.87—dc21   98-45159
                                                                  CIP
                                                                  AC

Note to Parents and Teachers

The Families series supports national social studies standards for units related to identifying family members and their roles in the family. This book describes and illustrates uncles and activities they do with their nieces and nephews. The photographs support emergent readers in understanding the text. The repetition of words and phrases helps emergent readers learn new words. This book also introduces emergent readers to subject-specific vocabulary words, which are defined in the Words to Know section. Emergent readers may need assistance to read some words and to use the Table of Contents, Words to Know, Read More, Internet Sites, and Index/Word List sections of the book.

Table of Contents

Uncles are brothers of mothers or fathers.

Uncles can have nieces.

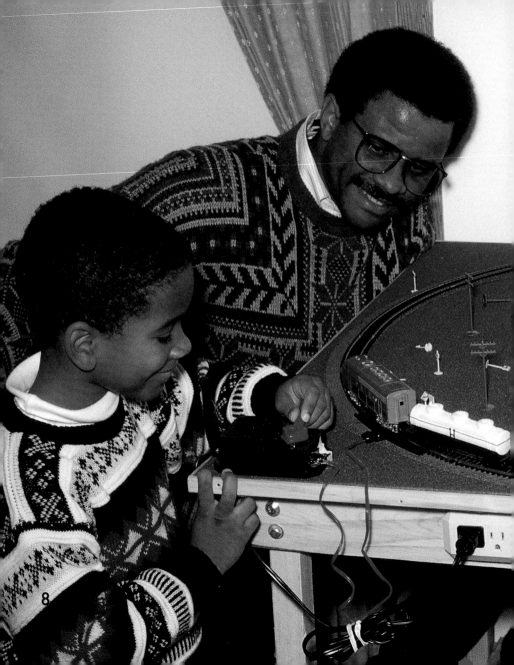

Uncles can have nephews.

Some uncles play
the guitar.

Some uncles hike.

Some uncles put
together puzzles.

Some uncles cook.

Some uncles jog.

Uncles listen.

Words to Know

brother—a boy or man who has the same parents as another person

guitar—a musical instrument people play by plucking or strumming its strings

hike—to go for a walk for fun or exercise

jog—to run at a slow pace

listen—to pay attention in order to hear something

nephew—the son of a person's brother or sister

niece—the daughter of a person's brother or sister

uncle—the brother of a person's mother or father; an uncle also can be the husband of a person's aunt.

Read More

Miller, Margaret. *Family Time.* A Super Chubby Board Book. New York: Little Simon, 1996.

Saunders-Smith, Gail. *Families.* People. Mankato, Minn.: Pebble Books, 1998.

Skutch, Robert. *Who's in a Family?* Berkeley, Calif.: Tricycle Press, 1995.

Internet Sites

Aunts and Uncles
http://www.firstct.com/fv/aunt.html

Family.com
http://family.go.com

Family First
http://hometown.aol.com/BMValen/index.html

Index/Word List

brothers, 5
cook, 17
fathers, 5
guitar, 11
hike, 13
jog, 19
listen, 21
mothers, 5

nephews, 9
nieces, 7
play, 11
put, 15
puzzles, 15
together, 15
uncles, 5, 7, 9, 11, 13, 15, 17, 19, 21

Word Count: 36
Early-Intervention Level: 5

Editorial Credits
Mari C. Schuh, editor; Steve Weil/Tandem Design, cover designer and illustrator; Kimberly Danger, photo researcher

Photo Credits
David F. Clobes, 4
Jim Cummins/FPG International LLC, 20
PhotoBank, Inc./Willie Holdman, 1; Mitch Diamond, 10
Photo Network/Tom McCarthy, 6; Myrleen Ferguson Cate, 16
Photri-Microstock, cover
Shaffer Photography/James L. Shaffer, 8
Unicorn Stock Photos/Karen Holsinger Mullen, 14; Aneal E. Vohra, 18
Visuals Unlimited, Jeff Greenberg, 12

Special thanks to Joy Allison, Lori Hollenback, and Penny McCarthy, first-grade teachers at Evergreen Primary in University Place, Washington, for reviewing the books in the Families series.